Easy Piano

# BERNSTEIN
## BROADWAY SONGS

### WEST SIDE STORY

ON THE TOWN

## 1600 PENNSYLVANIA AVENUE

# CANDIDE

Wonderful TOWN

ISBN 978-0-634-09754-0

LEONARD
BERNSTEIN
*Music Publishing*
Company LLC

## BOOSEY & HAWKES

An IMAGEM Company

DISTRIBUTED BY

HAL•LEONARD®
CORPORATION

7777 W. BLUEMOUND RD. P.O. BOX 13819 MILWAUKEE, WI 53213

www. Boosey.com

Visit Hal Leonard Online at
**www.halleonard.com**

# BERNSTEIN
## BROADWAY SONGS

4    **America**

7    **I Feel Pretty**

12    **A Little Bit in Love**

16    **Lonely Town**

26    **Make Our Garden Grow**

23    **Maria**

32    **New York, New York**

36    **Ohio**

39    **Some Other Time**

44    **Somewhere**

48    **Take Care of This House**

51    **Tonight**

# AMERICA
## from WEST SIDE STORY

Lyrics by Stephen Sondheim

Music by Leonard Bernstein
Arranged by Carol Klose

**Moderately bright**

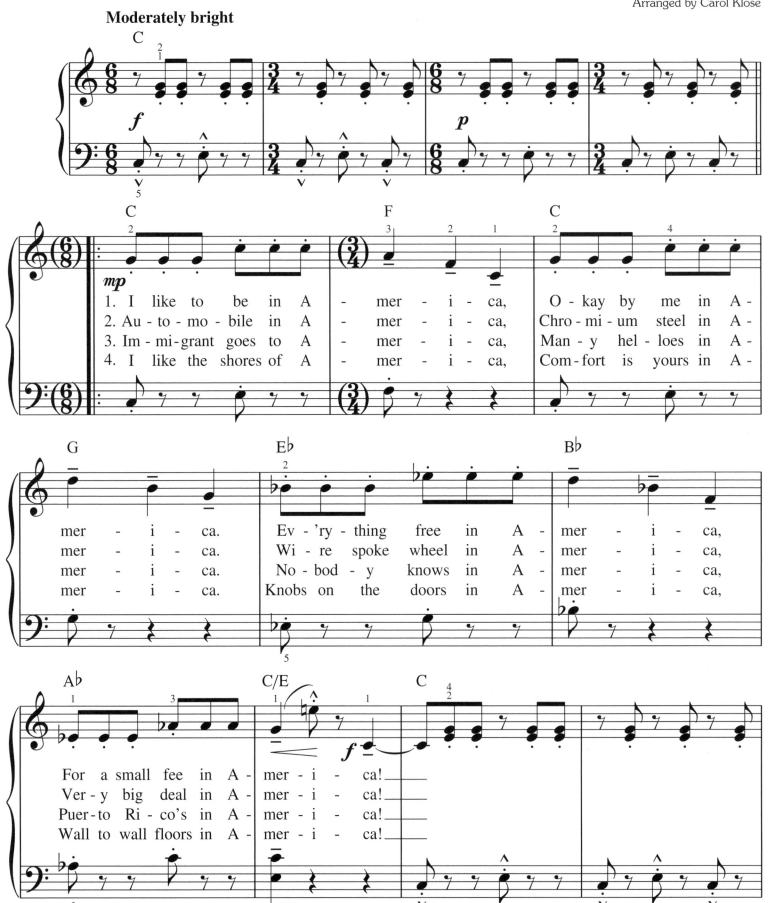

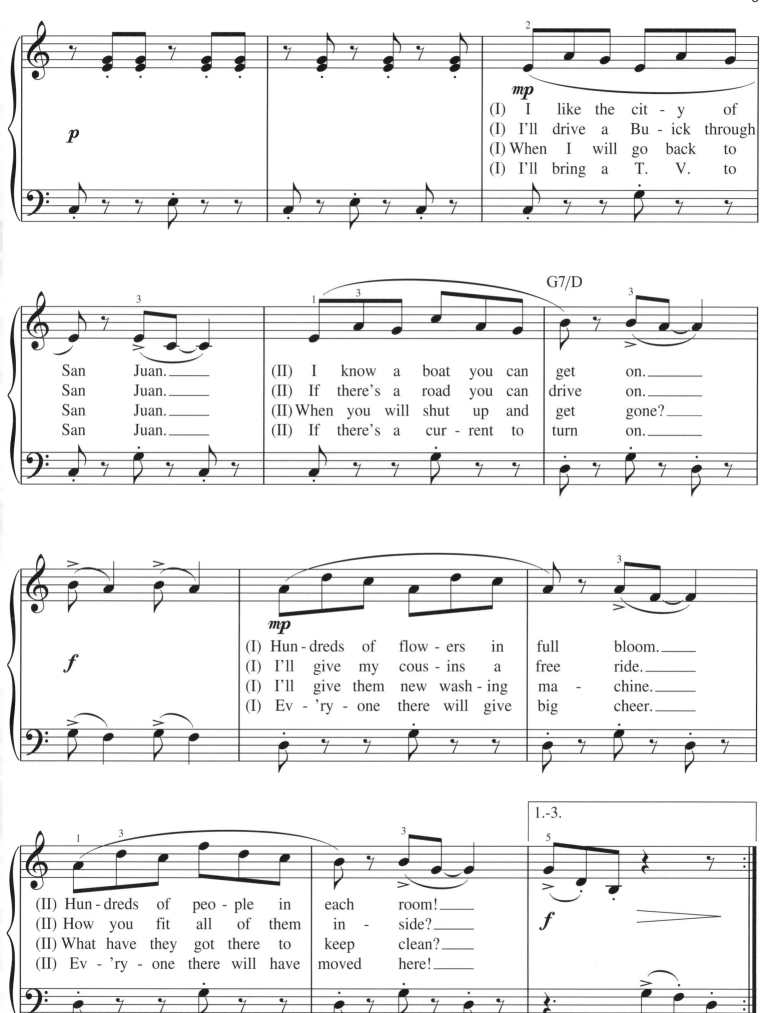

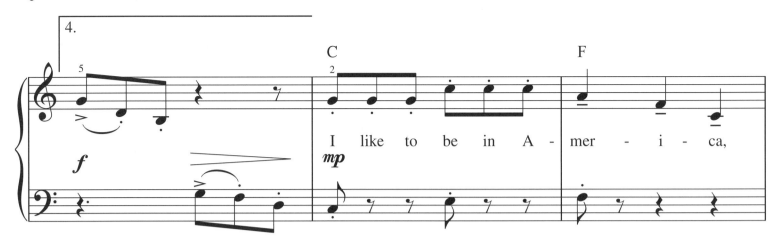

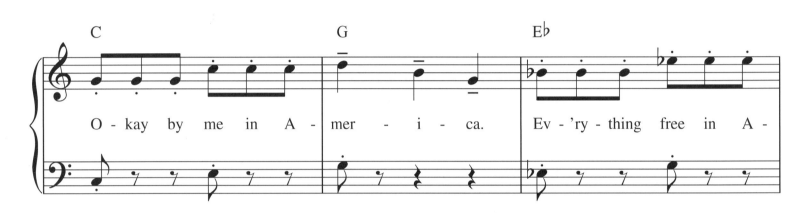

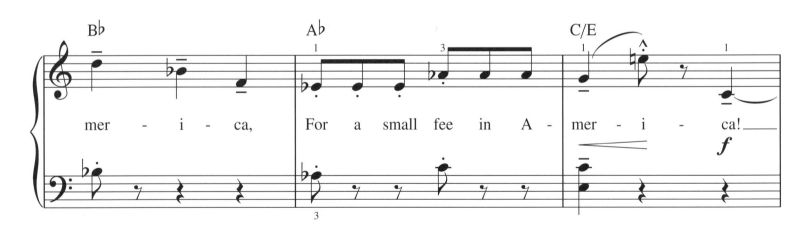

# I FEEL PRETTY

## from WEST SIDE STORY

Lyrics by Stephen Sondheim

Music by Leonard Bernstein
Arranged by Carol Klose

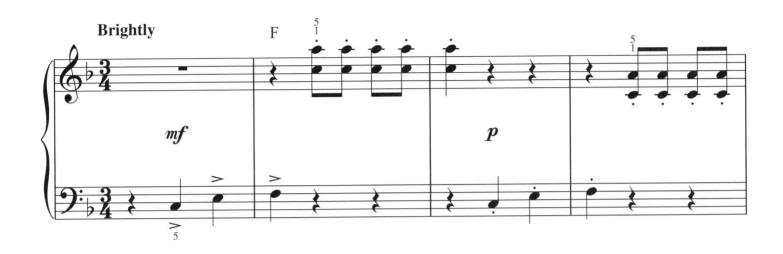

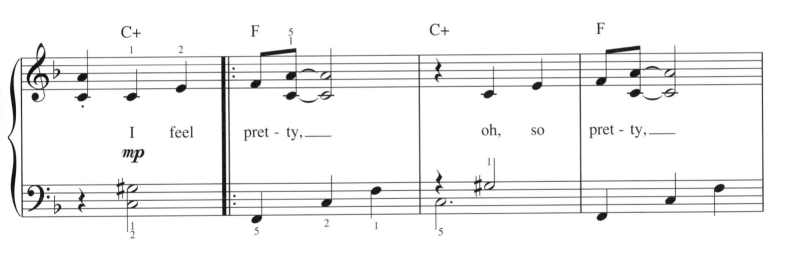

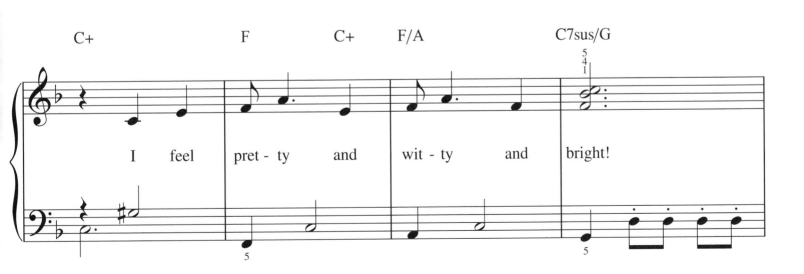

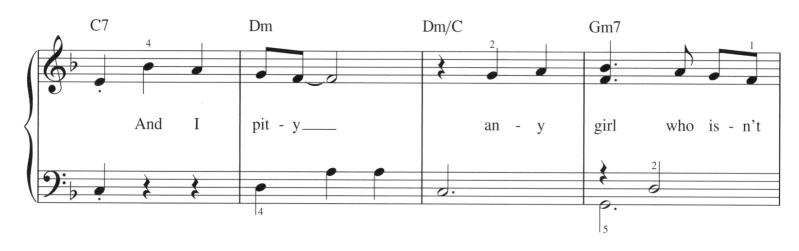

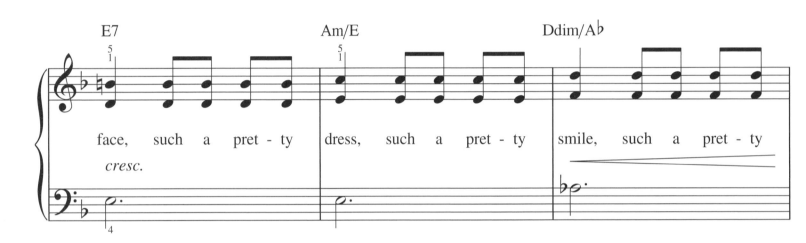

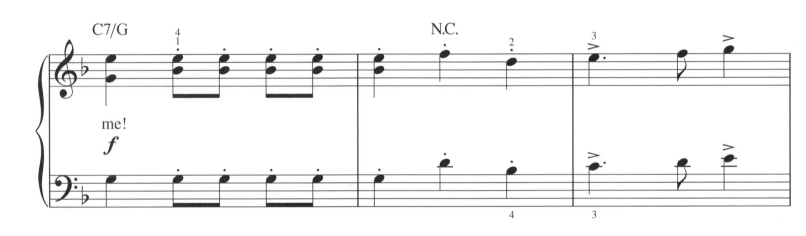

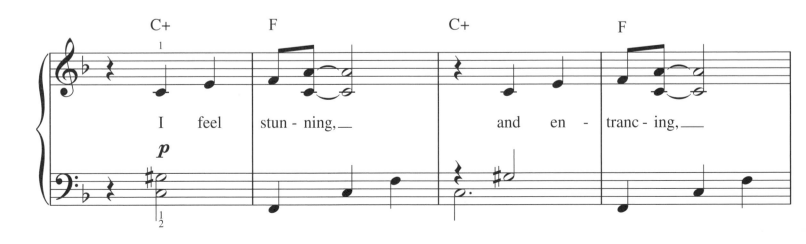

# A LITTLE BIT IN LOVE
### from WONDERFUL TOWN

Lyrics by Betty Comden
and Adolph Green

Music by Leonard Bernstein
Arranged by Rachel Chapin

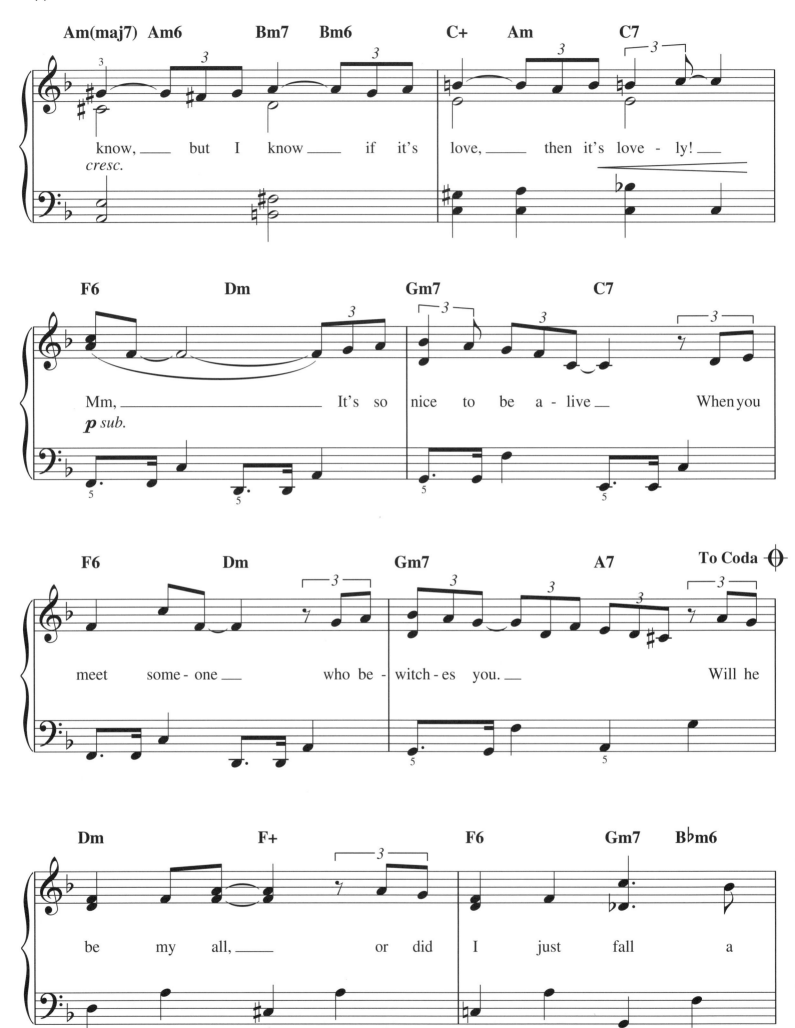

# LONELY TOWN

### from ON THE TOWN

Lyrics by Betty Comden
and Adolph Green

Music by Leonard Bernstein
Arranged by Rachel Chapin

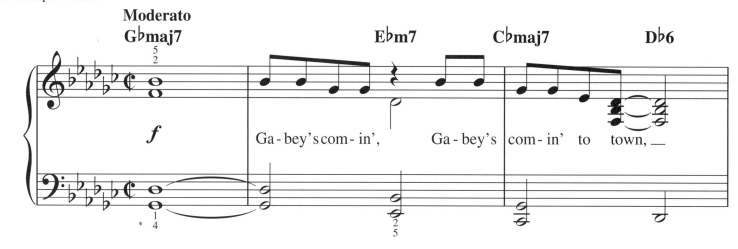

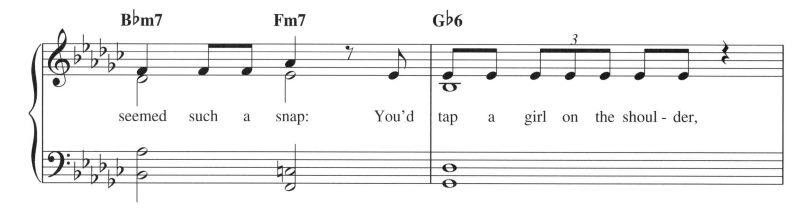

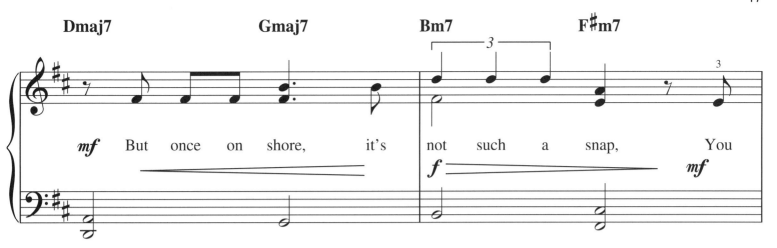

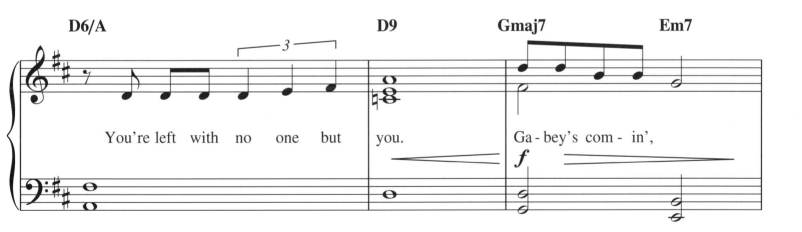

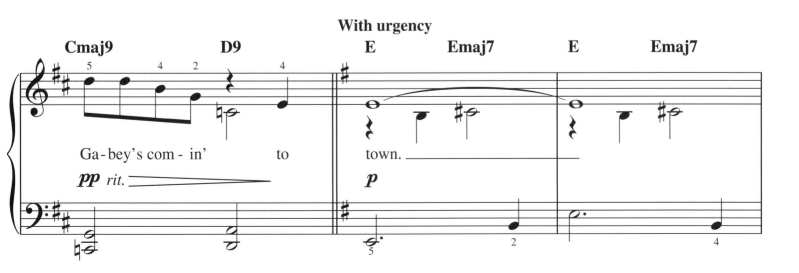

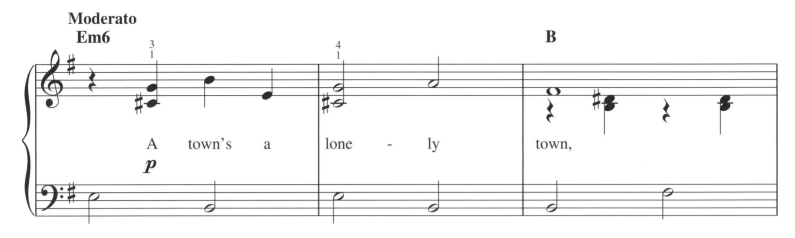

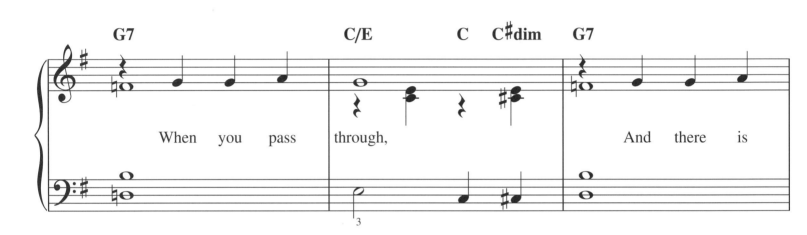

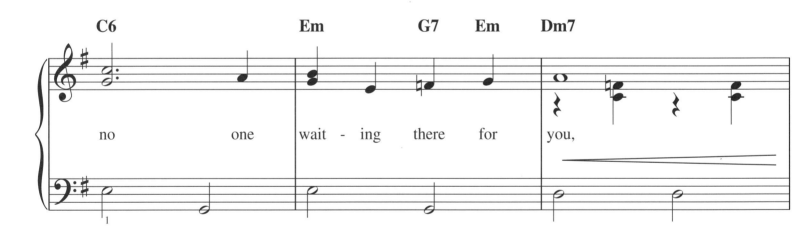

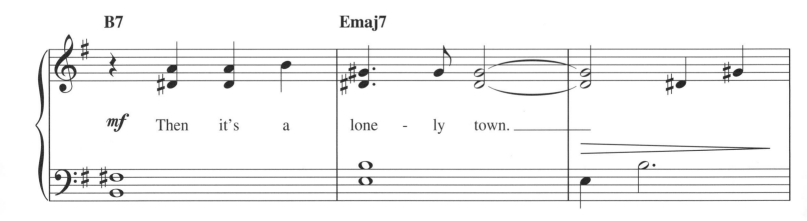

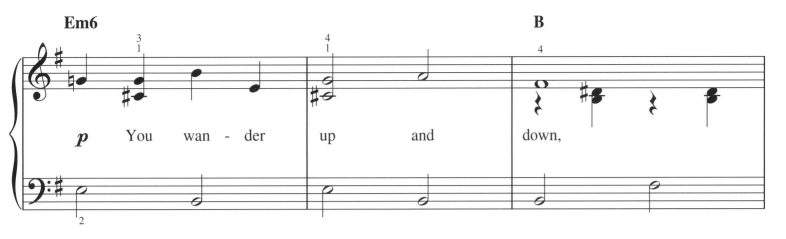

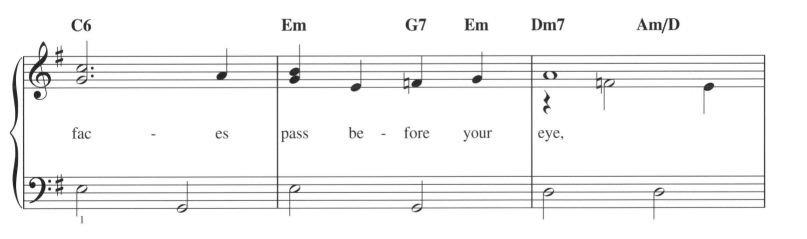

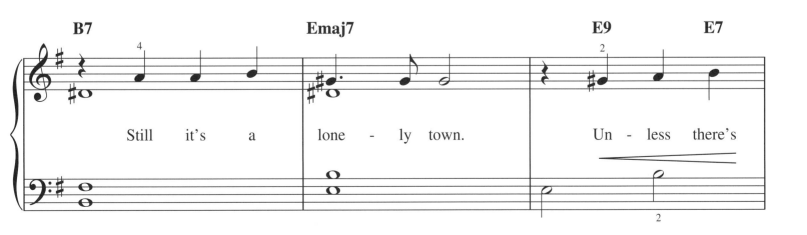

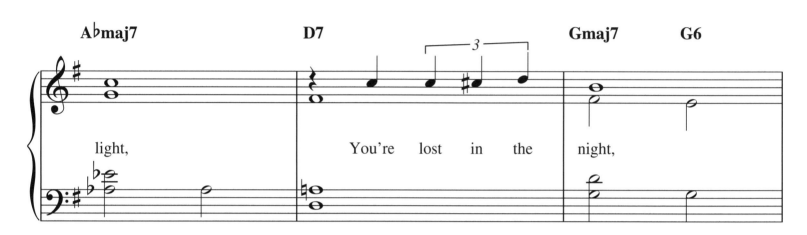

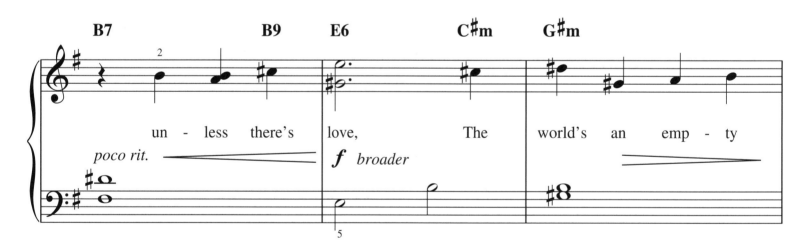

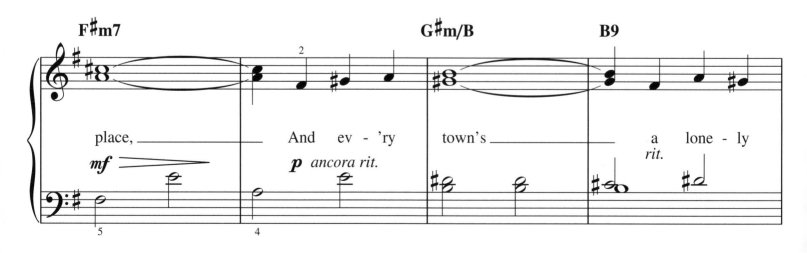

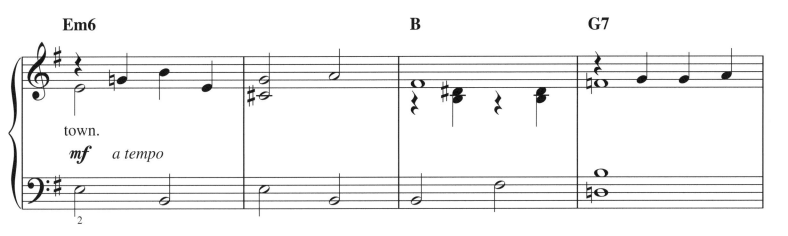

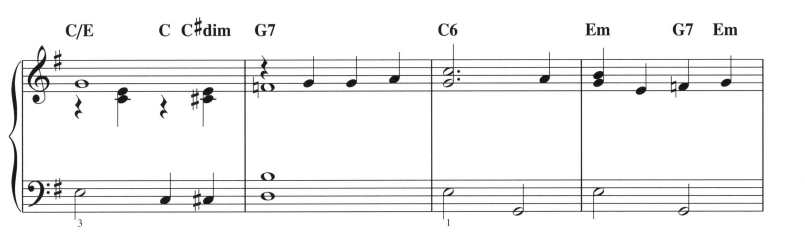

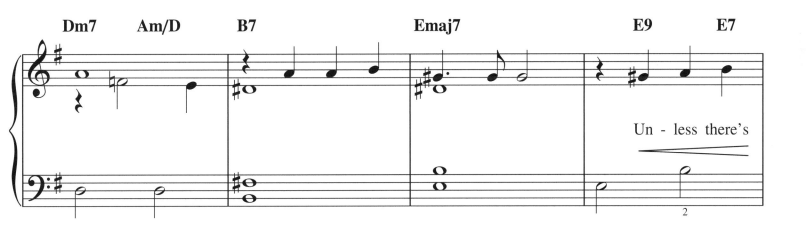

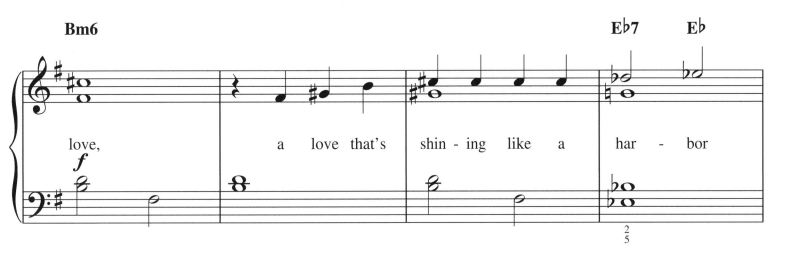

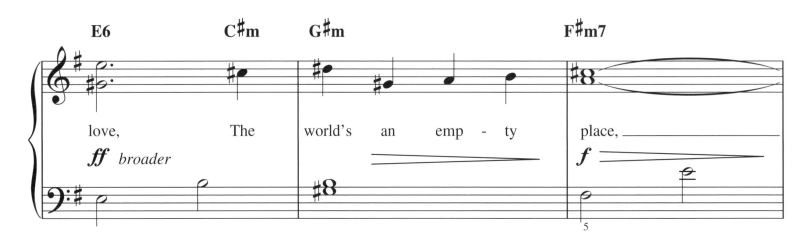

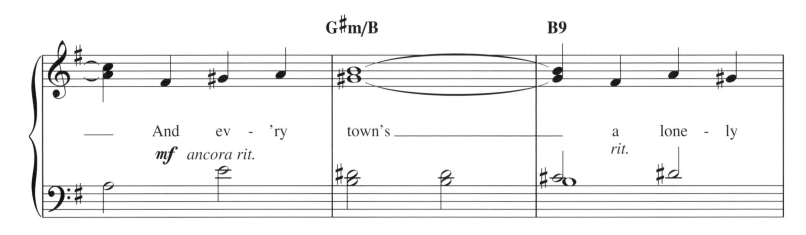

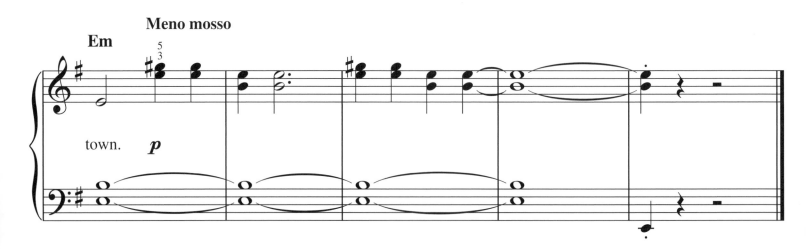

# MARIA
## from WEST SIDE STORY

Lyrics by Stephen Sondheim

Music by Leonard Bernstein
Arranged by Carol Klose

**Chorus**
**Moderately, with expression**

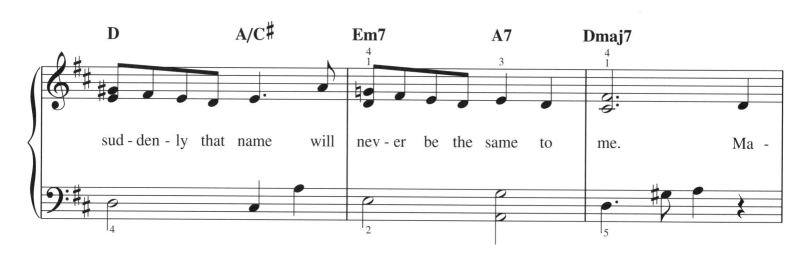

# MAKE OUR GARDEN GROW

**from CANDIDE**

Lyrics by Richard Wilbur

Music by Leonard Bernstein
Arranged by Rachel Chapin

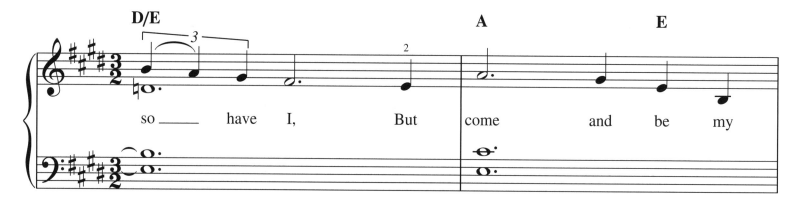

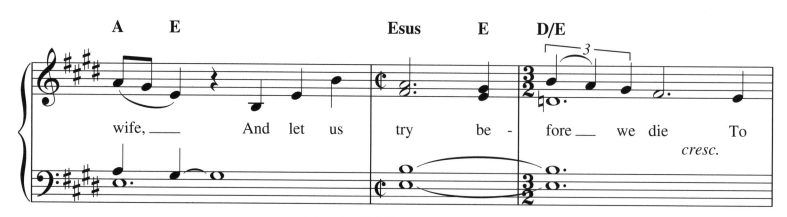

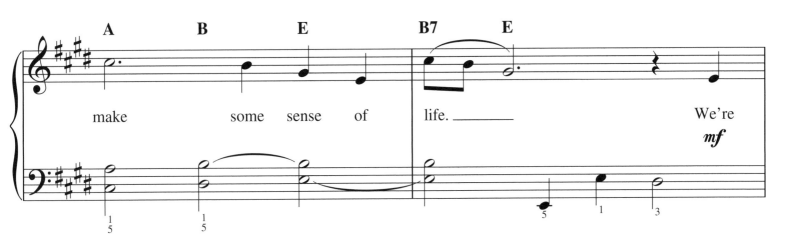

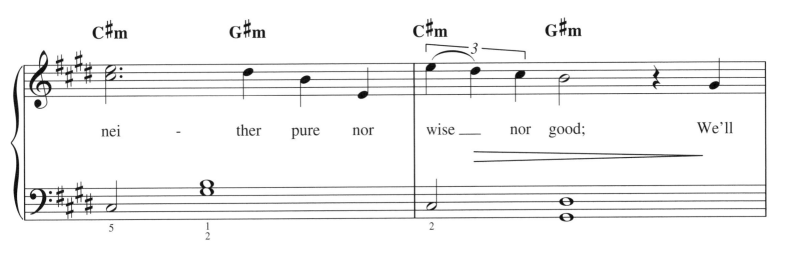

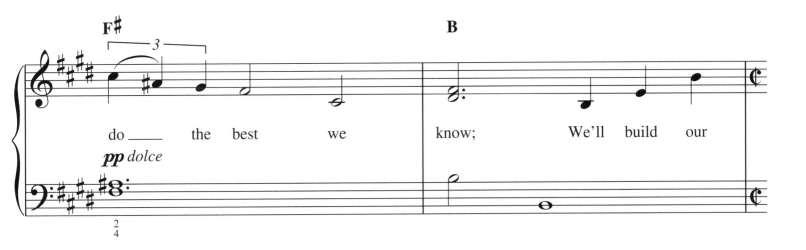

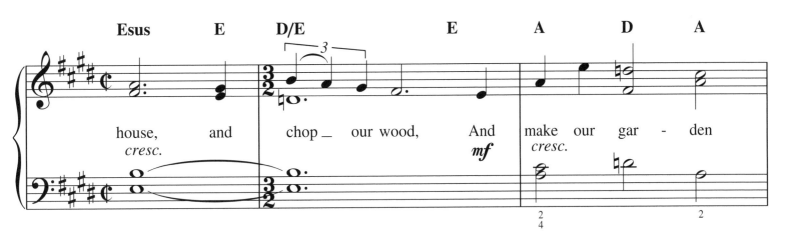

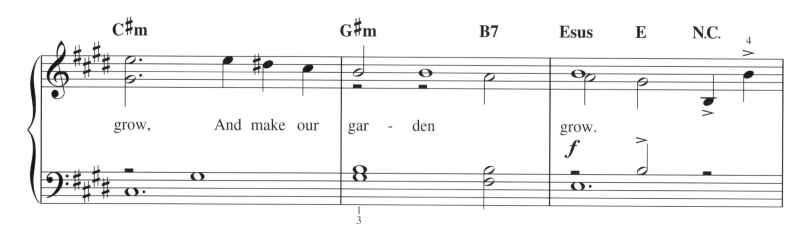

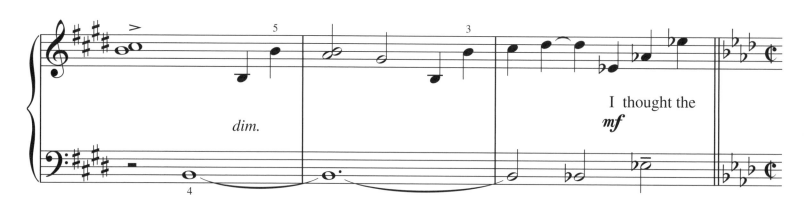

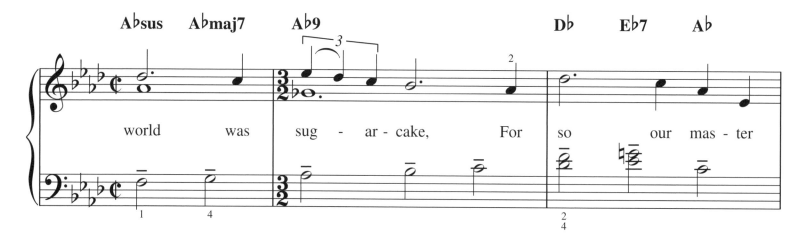

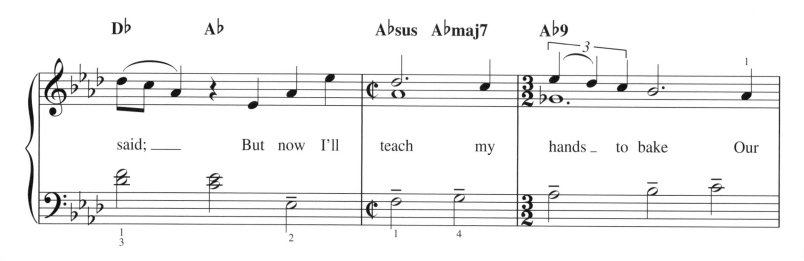

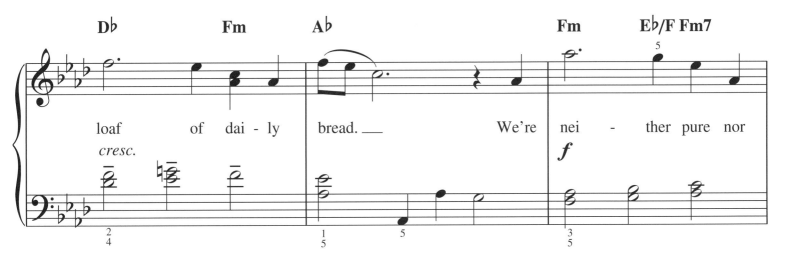

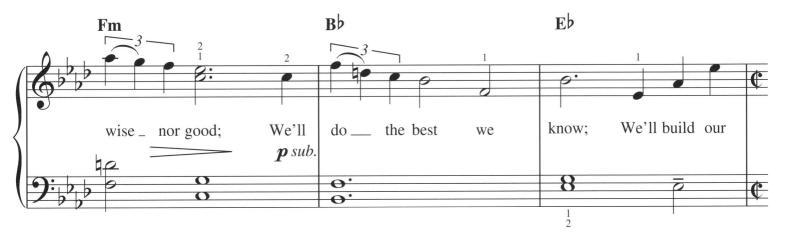

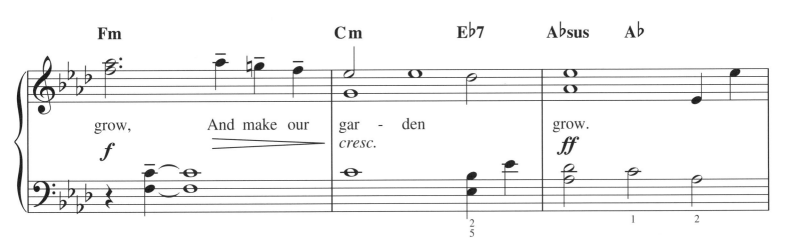

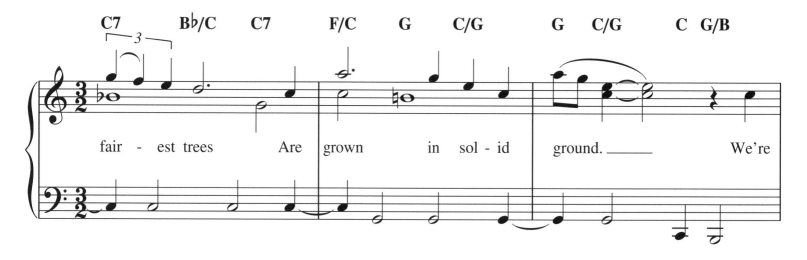

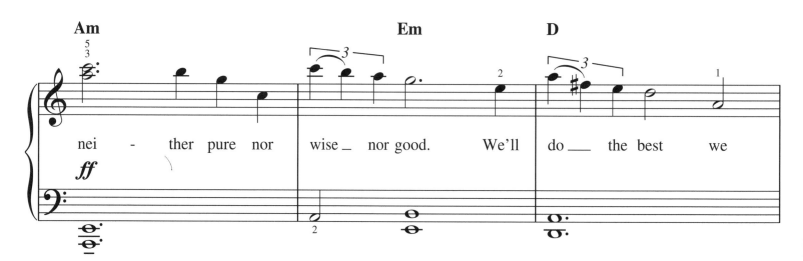

# NEW YORK, NEW YORK

**from ON THE TOWN**

Lyrics by Betty Comden
and Adolph Green

Music by Leonard Bernstein
Arranged by Rachel Chapin

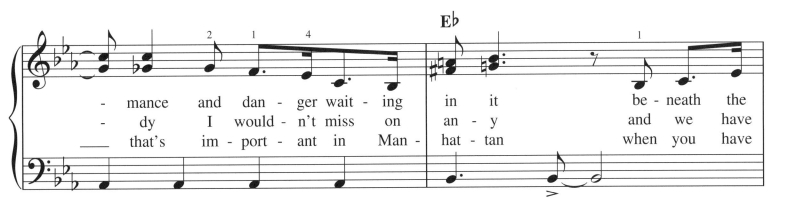

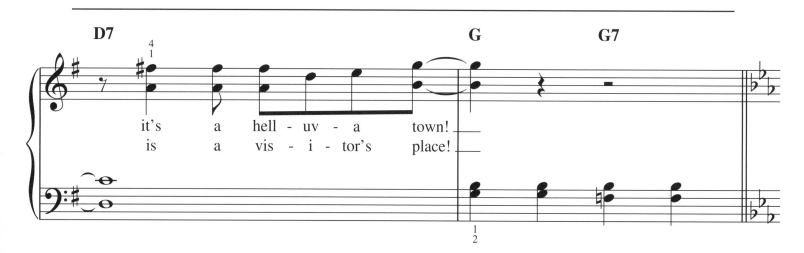

# OHIO
### from WONDERFUL TOWN

Lyrics by Betty Comden
and Adolph Green

Music by Leonard Bernstein
Arranged by Rachel Chapin

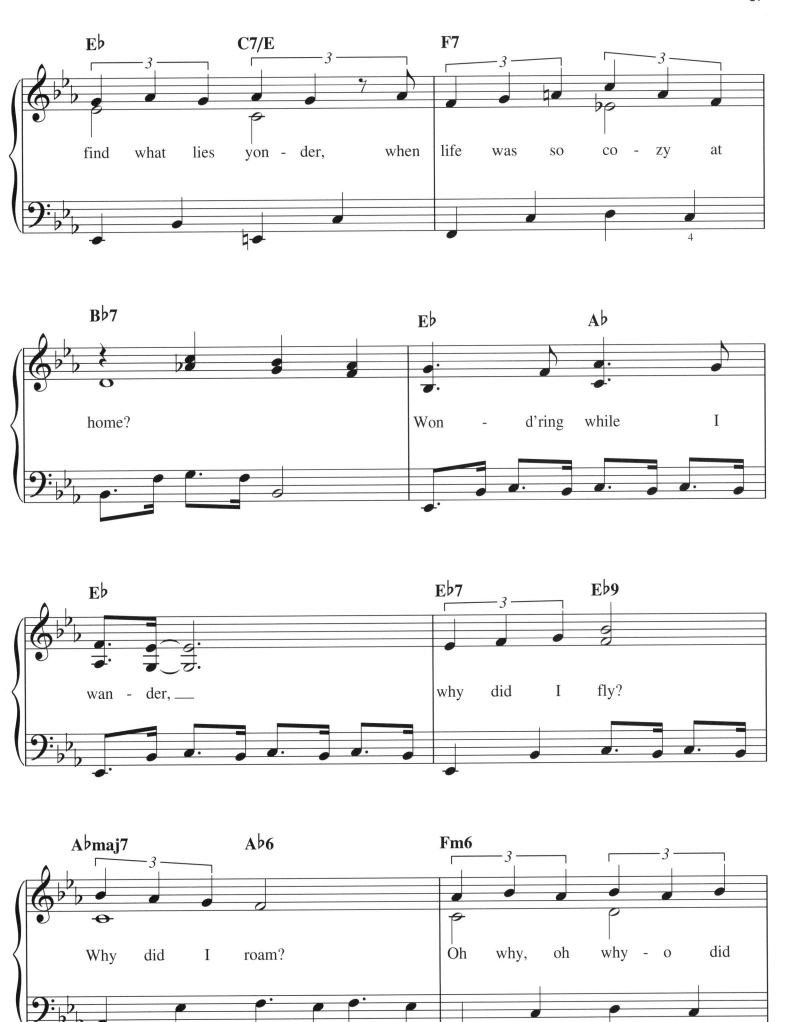

# SOME OTHER TIME

### from ON THE TOWN

Lyrics by Betty Comden
and Adolph Green

Music by Leonard Bernstein
Arranged by Rachel Chapin

**Freely, with sentiment**

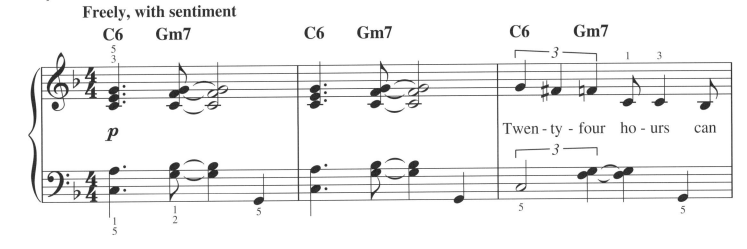

Twen - ty - four ho - urs can

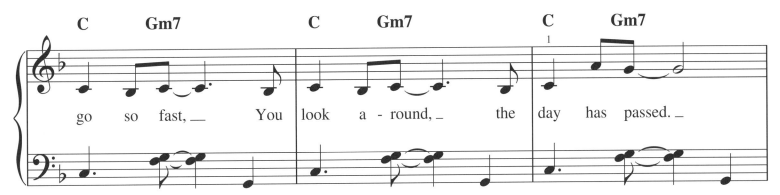

go so fast, __ You look a - round, __ the day has passed. __

When you're in love    Time is pre - cious stuff;    *rit.*    E - ven a life - time

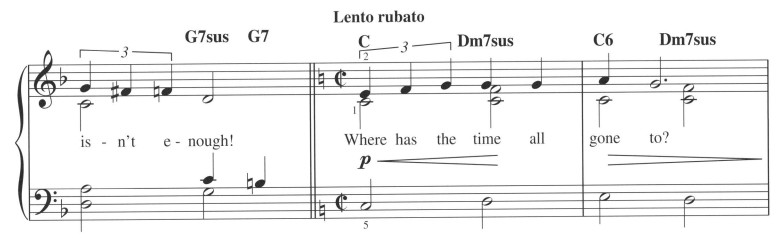

**Lento rubato**

is - n't e - nough!    Where has the time all    gone to?

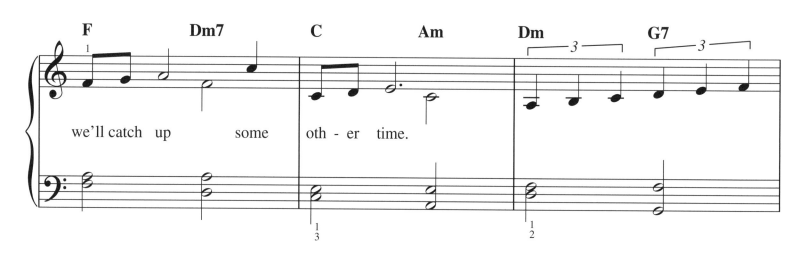

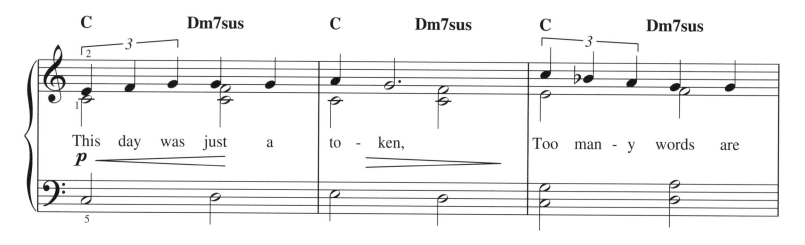

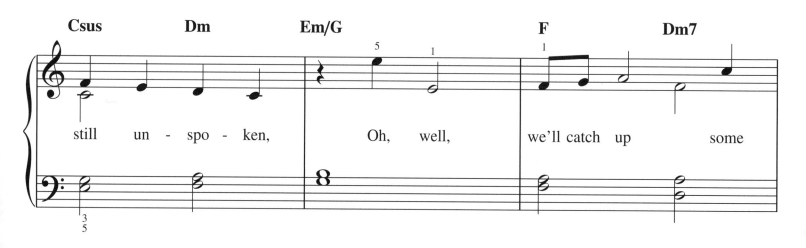

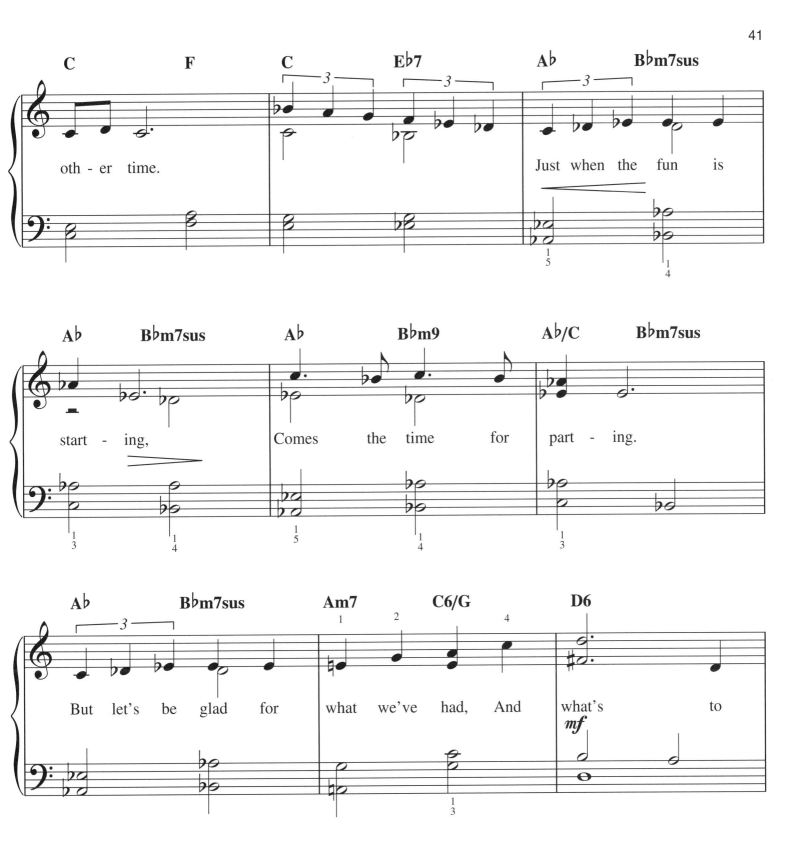

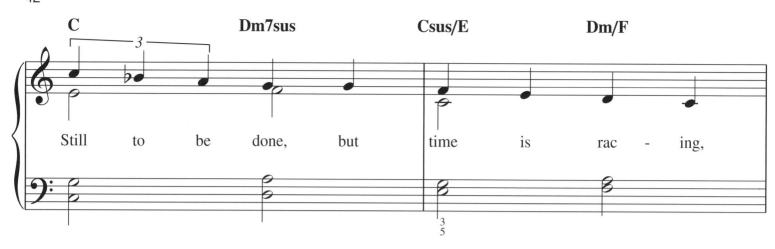

Still to be done, but time is rac - ing,

Oh, well, we'll catch up some oth - er time.

Just when the fun is

Comes the time for part - ing,

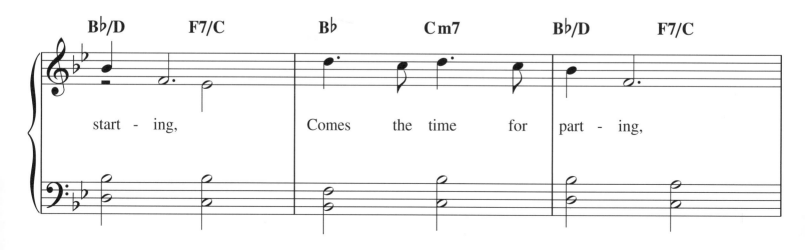

start - ing,

# SOMEWHERE
## from WEST SIDE STORY

Lyrics by Stephen Sondheim

Music by Leonard Bernstein
Arranged by Carol Klose

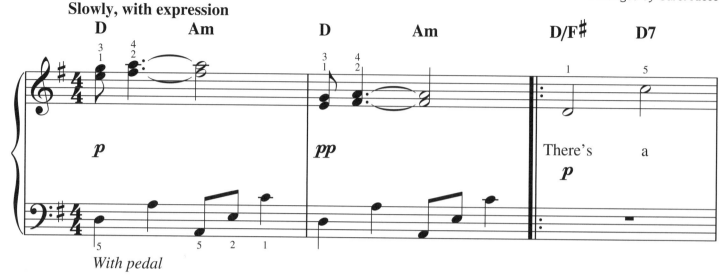

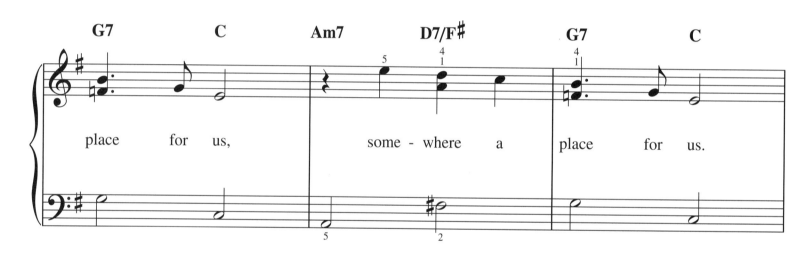

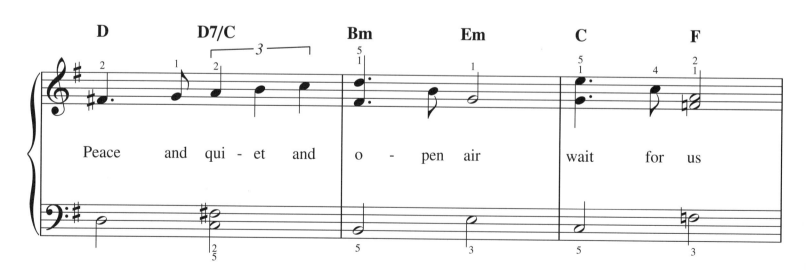

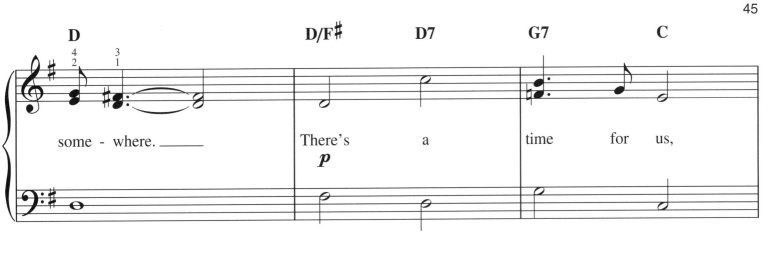

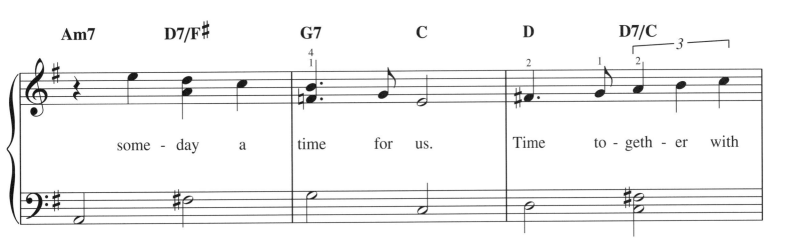

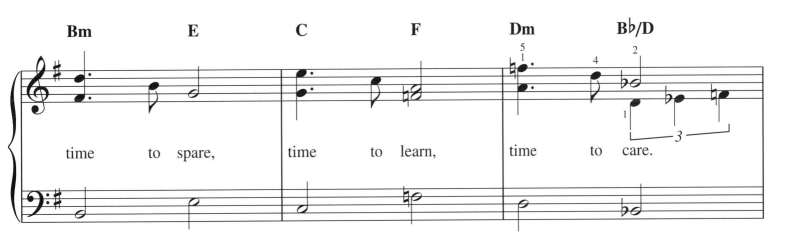

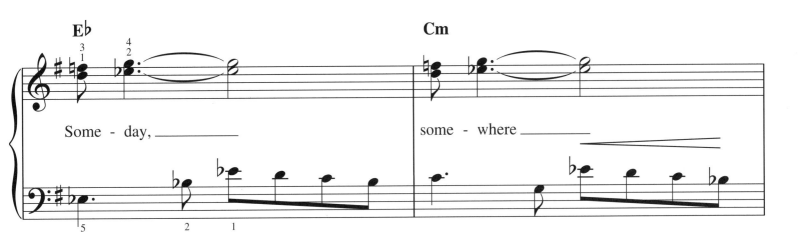

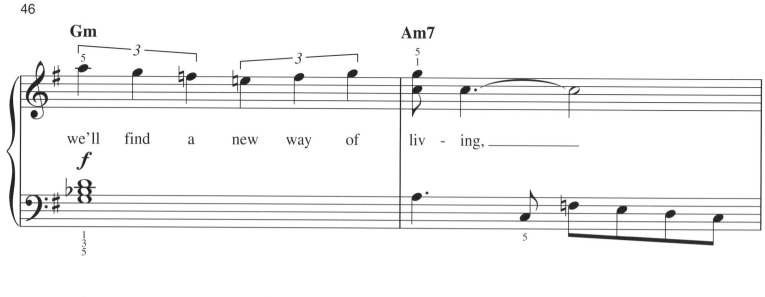

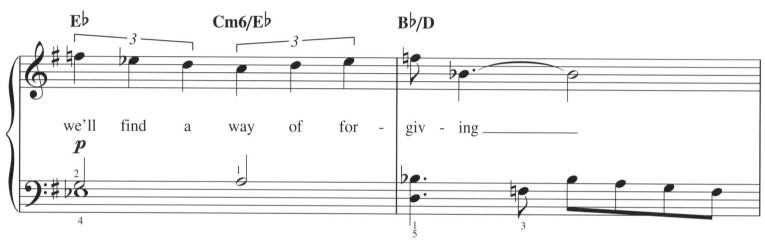

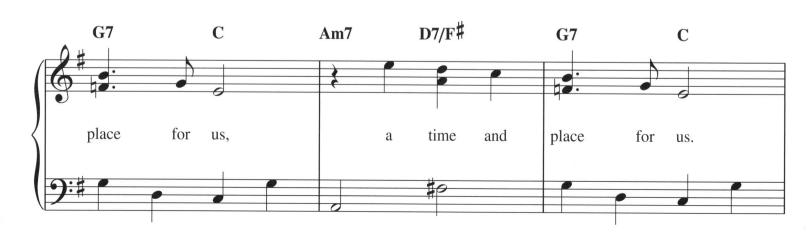

# TAKE CARE OF THIS HOUSE

from 1600 PENNSYLVANIA AVENUE

Lyrics by Alan Jay Lerner

Music by Leonard Bernstein
Arranged by Rachel Chapin

50

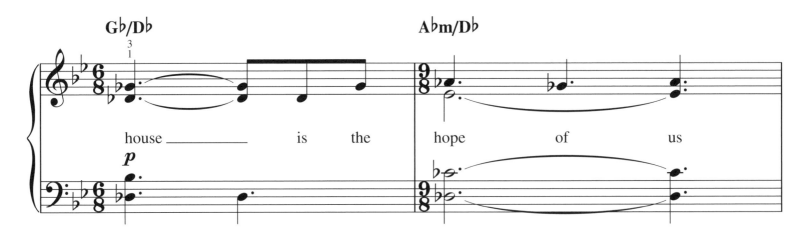

house _____ is the hope of us

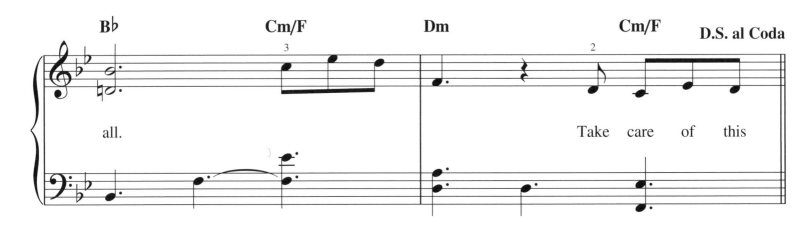

all. Take care of this

**D.S. al Coda**

**CODA**

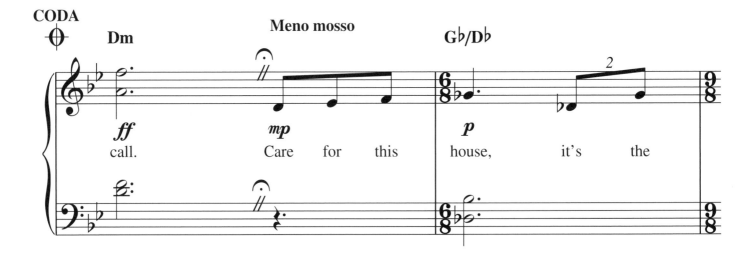

call. Care for this house, it's the

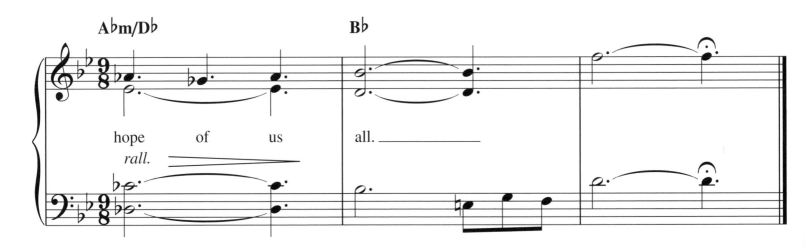

hope of us all. _____

# TONIGHT

## from WEST SIDE STORY

Lyrics by Stephen Sondheim

Music by Leonard Bernstein
Arranged by Carol Klose

Lyrics: To - night, to - night, won't be just an - y night. To - night there will be no morn - ing star. To -

night, to - night, I'll see my love to -

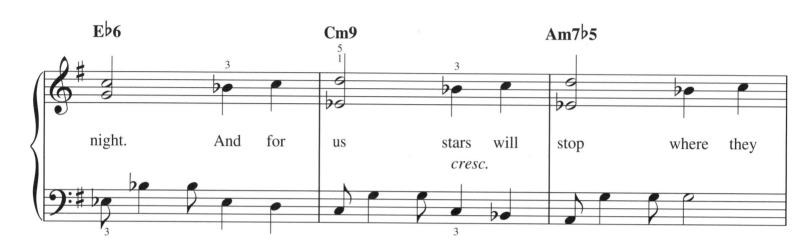

night. And for us stars will stop where they

*cresc.*

are! _____ To - day the min - utes seem like

*mf* *f*

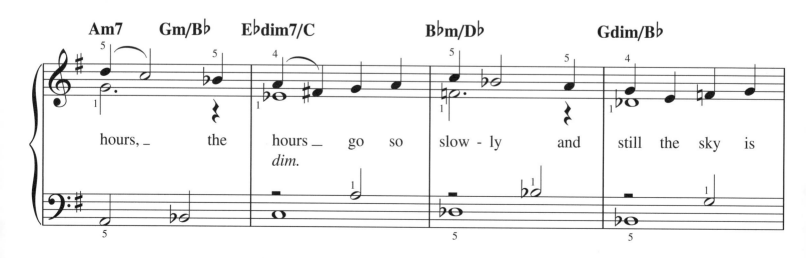

hours, \_ the hours \_ go so slow - ly and still the sky is

*dim.*